Past Experiences

WRITE 'EM DOWN

OUTDOOR TRAVEL RECORD

This personal trip record belongs to

_____

_____
Year

By Mike Rudarmel and Fran Sloan
AHA Calligraphy
&
QCC, Inc. Publishers
Portland, Oregon
©1993

Dedicated to our
fellow travelers - may your journal be
filled with memories of adventure and growth.
A special thanks to our partners, Ron Sloan and
Barbara Brunckhorst. Also to Lee Garrison, Chris Brunckhorst, and
Sarah Rudarmel for their help with
this book.

© 1993
QCC, Inc. & AHA Calligraphy
P.O. Box 2128
Beaverton, OR 97075 - 2128

All rights reserved
No part of this book may be reproduced without written
permission from the publishers.

ISBN 1-880133-39-3
Manufactured in the United States of America

Original watercolor on cover
& calligraphy by Fran Sloan

Plant & Animal graphics courtesy of
Dover Publications, Inc, Clip Art Series,
31 East 2nd street, Mineola N.Y. 11501

Printing by Bridgetown Printers, Portland, Oregon

PERSONAL INFORMATION

Name ─────────────────────────────
Address ─────────────────────────────
─────────────────────────────
Phone ─────────────────────────────
─────────────────────────────

Social Security Number ─────────────────
Driver's License Number ─────────────────
Passport / Visa Number ─────────────────
Travelers Checks ────────────────────
─────────────────────────────
─────────────────────────────

Credit Card Phone Numbers ─────────────────

In Case of Emergency Please Notify
Name ─────────────────────────────
Address ─────────────────────────────
─────────────────────────────
Phone ─────────────────────────────
─────────────────────────────
─────────────────────────────

Medical Information

Blood Type ─────────────────────────
Medic Alert ─────────────────────────
Physician ─────────────────────────
Phone ─────────────────────────────
─────────────────────────────

Allergies ─────────────────────────
Other important information ─────────────

In America, there are two classes of TRAVEL: first class & with children.

Robert Benchley

CONTENTS

	PAGES
INTRODUCTION	6-7
INFORMATION	
Guide for Successful Travel	8-9
How to Use This Book	10-11
TRAVEL RECORD	12-59
Basic Trip Log & Journal	
JOURNAL PAGES	60-83
Extended Description & Keepsakes	
TRIP PLANNER-ITINERARY	85-93
Detailed Pre-trip Organization	
CALENDAR	95
Order Information	96

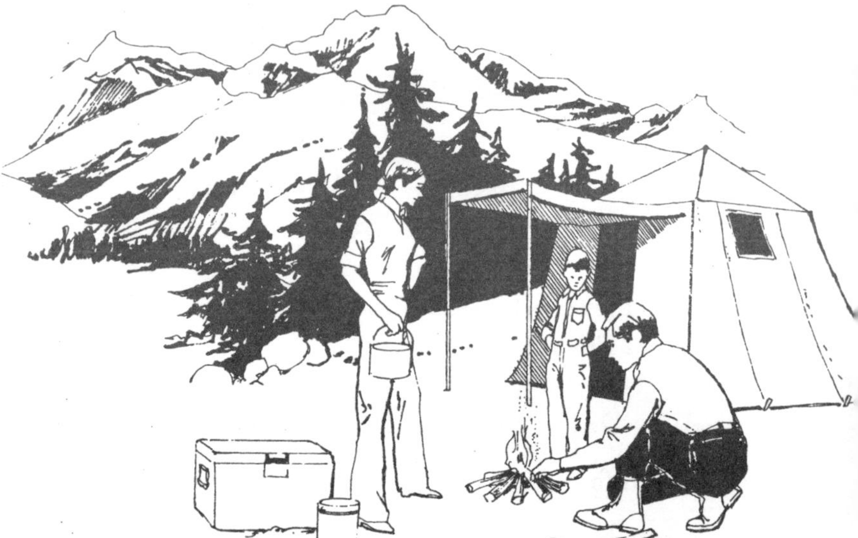

INTRODUCTION

We've all had vacations or trips that were worth remembering. Many have been "PEAK EXPERIENCES". Sometimes our memories dim when recalling the events.

Mike was planning his hike to the summit of Mt. Hood and looked for a record like this one. None were available with formatting that fit his needs. He also wanted a good place to write about day hikes, weekend trips and longer travels. His partner, Barbara, has kept good records of their trips. This has proved to be invaluable when looking at photographs with family and friends.

Fran enjoys the process of journalizing because it slows her down and keeps her in the moment. Writing is fun for her. Fran's husband, Ron, says recording the trip experiences helps clear his thinking. Planning well organizes each trip and reduces frustration.

Traveling with children can be a great adventure with lots of events in a short time. Life moves along so quickly that we sometimes loose sight of wondrous peak experiences - often many in a single day! Write about it now and later, you and your family can recall peak experiences together.

We created this book to meet all our needs. When we decided to publish, we included wildlife images & quotations in calligraphy for your enjoyment. The main sections are:
   1. TRAVEL RECORD
   2. JOURNAL
   3. TRIP PLANNER

This outdoor travel record preserves events which helps you vividly recall your travels and keep all this valuable information in one place! For day trips or longer vacations, this book is for your use....take it with you!

Enjoy your travels!

Mike & Fran

Guide for Successful Travel

Here are a few things to consider when preparing for a trip. Making a check list for each of these general items can help avoid the dilemma of forgetting things, over packing, and loss of security at home. Take a look at the following and decide what is important for your travels:

Budget / Finances	How much is it going to cost and how will the money be handled.
Clothing	Pack for how many days? What's the weather forecast where you're going? Plan for the unexpected.
Equipment	Any special equipment for this trip? Know how your equipment works. Can you take everything apart and put it back together? Can you fix it if it breaks?
Food Preparation	Eating out, self-preparation, or a combination. Plan each meal by the day.
Home Security	Check all windows and doors. Local police have good home security check lists. Who will water your yard or house plants? Turn off hot water.
Pet Arrangements	Boarding, feeding and all of that.

Itinerary	Use the Trip Planner (pgs. 86-93) for longer trips. Make your schedule loose, tight, or both. Let someone know your plans and expected return.
Lodging	Make reservations and keep the relevant information at hand.
_____	_____
Inform Others	Leave itineraries with friends, relatives, or trusted neighbors. Have them keep an eye on things.
Deliveries	Arrange to have newspapers and mail collected daily or put on hold.

MAKE YOUR LIST

    A good planning list is invaluable. Brainstorm with your traveling companions. Share the jobs so everyone gets to help prepare for the trip.

    After you make your lists, put them aside for a time. Later, take another look at them. Travel light and emphasize the traveling and not the belongings. If something is forgotten, decide how important it is and either go back or leave it behind and put it far from your mind.

    When you've come up with a good list, write it down in your travel record to help prepare for the next trip.

A tip for the wise traveler:
**REMEMBER TO TAKE HALF THE CLOTHES
& TWICE THE MONEY!**

How to Use This Book

The samples below are guides for using the Travel Record and Journal. They document a weekend trip. These pages are helpful for all your trips. If you need more journal space, continue on the extended pages that begin on page 62 and note the page number.

For longer travels, you may use several of the Travel Records plus the Trip Planner - Itinerary pages that begin on page 85. These pages are most valuable for keeping all the important numbers - for reservations, dates, times - for

---

Page 12

TRAVEL RECORD

My Trip To *Lost Lake USFS Campground*

Description *Weekend tent trailer camping trip.*

Dates *6/25/93* (Leave)   *6/27/93* (Return)

Weather *Sunny and warm 1st two days - cloudy & windy with some rain on last day.*

Mode of Travel *Trooper*   Mileage *87*

Companions *Barbara, Chris, Mike & Sarah*

Leader/Sponsor _____

Places Visited *Took the scenic drive around south side of Mt. Hood to Lost Lake. Gorgeous! Route around other side (I-84) would have saved about 1 hour travel. Stopped in Hood River on way way home for snack.*

Memorable Events *Process of finding the perfect campsite. The reflection of Mt. Hood on the still waters of Lost Lake. Especially at night. Sarah's first clearly seeing the constellations.*

Wildlife Sightings *Bald Eagles fishing in lake. Near-tame campground chipmunks & a mass invasion of flying ants.*

Expenses *(Lodging/Dining/Fees)* *$12 camping fee. All day row boat rental for $25.00*

Surprises *The rain on the tent Saturday night sounded just like a rain stick.*

Itinerary for this trip is on page *na*   Journal continued on page *63*

names and details you'll need on your travels. Note the page number at the bottom of the Travel Record.

Date this journal with a waterproof marker on the line provided on the spine of this book. You'll easily find it on your bookshelf years later when you want to recall these peak experiences.

Keep this book with you constantly. Put it in your backpack, glove box or pocket. We've provided a format that gives you flexibility and structure. This is your book... keep good notes that you can enjoy for years to come.

Journal

We are surprised at how close this beautiful spot is to Portland and that none of us had been here before. Half the campsites that were available were by the Lake. Most of the lake sites are isolated. There are many new sites under construction above the Lake. General store, boats & cabins w/o water for rent.

Friday was a gorgeous sunny day. Not only was the sun out but so were all the BUGS that hadn't hatched all year. No water shortage this year! Some bugs looked like flying carpenter ants. They divebombed us all day!

We rented a rowboat for fishing on the second day. Just as we started fishing the wind came up. We had a few bites but no fish for dinner. The stock truck had loaded 10,000 fish in the lake the day before but they must have been hanging out on the bottom which is about 167' deep. We'll be back next summer.

We tied the boat up just below our campground. Everyone had a turn at rowing.

There is a three mile trail around the lake and about 3/8 of a mile is boardwalk over the marsh area. A night heron flew right by us! A nature tour was

TRAVEL RECORD

My Trip To _____

Description _____
_____

Dates _____
           Leave   Return

Weather _____
_____

Mode of Travel _____ Mileage _____

Companions _____
_____

Leader/Sponsor _____

Places Visited _____
_____
_____
_____

Memorable Events _____
_____
_____
_____

Wildlife Sightings _____
_____
_____

Expenses *(Lodging/Dining/Fees)* _____
_____
_____

Surprises _____
_____
_____

Itinerary for this trip is on page _____   Journal contunued on page _____

Journal

TRAVEL RECORD

My Trip To _____

Description _____
_____

Dates _____
            Leave   Return
Weather _____
_____

Mode of Travel _____ Mileage _____

Companions _____
_____

Leader/Sponsor _____

Places Visited _____
_____
_____
_____

Memorable Events _____
_____
_____
_____

Wildlife Sightings _____
_____
_____

Expenses *(Lodging/Dining/Fees)* _____
_____
_____
_____   _____

Surprises _____
_____
_____

Itinerary for this trip is on page _____   **Journal contunued on page** _____

Journal

I am glad I shall never be young without **WILD COUNTRY** *to be young in. Of what avail are forty freedoms without a blank spot on the map*

—Aldo Leopold

TRAVEL RECORD

My Trip To _____

Description_____
_____

Dates_____
            Leave   Return
Weather_____
_____

Mode of Travel _____ Mileage_____

Companions_____
_____

Leader/Sponsor_____

Places Visited_____
_____
_____
_____

Memorable Events_____
_____
_____
_____

Wildlife Sightings_____
_____
_____

Expenses *(Lodging/Dining/Fees)*_____
_____
_____
_____

Surprises_____
_____
_____

Itinerary for this trip is on page _____   **Journal contunued on page _____**

Journal

Foxglove

TRAVEL RECORD

My Trip To _____

Description _____
_____

Dates _____
            Leave   Return

Weather _____
_____

Mode of Travel _____ Mileage _____

Companions _____
_____

Leader/Sponsor _____

Places Visited _____
_____
_____
_____

Memorable Events _____
_____
_____
_____

Wildlife Sightings _____
_____
_____

Expenses *(Lodging/Dining/Fees)* _____
_____
_____
_____

Surprises _____
_____
_____

Itinerary for this trip is on page _____   Journal contunued on page _____

Journal

> Forget not that the *earth delights* to feel your bare feet & the winds long to play with your hair.
>
> — Kahlil Gibran

# TRAVEL RECORD

My Trip To _____

Description _____
_____

Dates _____
       Leave   Return
Weather _____
_____

Mode of Travel _____ Mileage _____

Companions _____
_____

Leader/Sponsor _____

Places Visited _____
_____
_____
_____

Memorable Events _____
_____
_____
_____

Wildlife Sightings _____
_____
_____

Expenses *(Lodging/Dining/Fees)* _____
_____
_____

Surprises _____
_____
_____

Itinerary for this trip is on page _____   Journal contunued on page _____

Journal

Raccoon

TRAVEL RECORD

My Trip To _____

Description _____
_____

Dates _____
           Leave   Return
Weather _____
_____

Mode of Travel _____ Mileage _____

Companions _____
_____

Leader/Sponsor _____

Places Visited _____
_____
_____
_____

Memorable Events _____
_____
_____
_____

Wildlife Sightings _____
_____
_____

Expenses *(Lodging/Dining/Fees)* _____
_____
_____
_____

Surprises _____
_____
_____

Itinerary for this trip is on page _____   Journal contunued on page _____

Journal

> It furthers one to
> have somewhere
> to go. — I Ching

TRAVEL RECORD

My Trip To _____

Description _____
_____

Dates _____
             Leave   Return
Weather _____
_____

Mode of Travel _____ Mileage _____

Companions _____
_____

Leader/Sponsor _____

Places Visited _____
_____
_____
_____

Memorable Events _____
_____
_____
_____

Wildlife Sightings _____
_____
_____

Expenses *(Lodging/Dining/Fees)* _____
_____
_____

Surprises _____
_____
_____

Itinerary for this trip is on page _____   Journal contunued on page _____

Journal

Columbine

TRAVEL RECORD

My Trip To _____

Description _____
_____

Dates _____
           Leave   Return
Weather _____
_____

Mode of Travel _____ Mileage _____

Companions _____
_____

Leader/Sponsor _____

Places Visited _____
_____
_____
_____

Memorable Events _____
_____
_____
_____
_____

Wildlife Sightings _____
_____
_____

Expenses *(Lodging/Dining/Fees)* _____
_____
_____
_____

Surprises _____
_____
_____

Itinerary for this trip is on page _____   Journal contunued on page _____

Journal

> In the midst of winter,
> I finally learned that
> there was in me an invincible
> **Summer**
>
> — Albert Camus

TRAVEL RECORD

My Trip To _____

Description _____
_____

Dates _____
            Leave   Return
Weather _____
_____

Mode of Travel _____ Mileage _____

Companions _____
_____

Leader/Sponsor _____

Places Visited _____
_____
_____
_____

Memorable Events _____
_____
_____
_____
_____

Wildlife Sightings _____
_____
_____

Expenses *(Lodging/Dining/Fees)* _____
_____
_____

Surprises _____
_____
_____

Itinerary for this trip is on page _____   Journal contunued on page _____

Journal

Mountain Goat

Page 30

TRAVEL RECORD

My Trip To _____

Description _____
_____

Dates _____
        Leave   Return
Weather _____
_____

Mode of Travel _____ Mileage _____

Companions _____
_____

Leader/Sponsor _____

Places Visited _____
_____
_____
_____

Memorable Events _____
_____
_____
_____

Wildlife Sightings _____
_____
_____

Expenses *(Lodging/Dining/Fees)* _____
_____
_____
_____

Surprises _____
_____
_____

Itinerary for this trip is on page _____   **Journal contunued on page _____**

Journal

If *flies* did not annoy people, the world would be covered with flies.

Anon.

Page 32

TRAVEL RECORD

My Trip To _____

Description_____
_____

Dates_____
           Leave   Return
Weather_____
_____

Mode of Travel _____ Mileage_____

Companions_____
_____

Leader/Sponsor_____

Places Visited_____
_____
_____
_____

Memorable Events_____
_____
_____
_____

Wildlife Sightings_____
_____
_____

Expenses *(Lodging/Dining/Fees)*_____
_____
_____

Surprises_____
_____
_____

Itinerary for this trip is on page _____   Journal contunued on page _____

Journal

TRAVEL RECORD

My Trip To _____

Description _____
_____

Dates _____
           Leave   Return
Weather _____
_____

Mode of Travel _____ Mileage _____

Companions _____
_____

Leader/Sponsor _____

Places Visited _____
_____
_____
_____

Memorable Events _____
_____
_____
_____

Wildlife Sightings _____
_____
_____

Expenses *(Lodging/Dining/Fees)* _____
_____
_____
_____

Surprises _____
_____
_____

Itinerary for this trip is on page _____   **Journal contunued on page** _____

Journal

> One touch of NATURE makes the whole world kin.
>
> *Shakespeare*

Page 36

TRAVEL RECORD

My Trip To _____

Description_____
_____

Dates_____
    Leave   Return
Weather_____
_____

Mode of Travel _____ Mileage_____

Companions_____
_____

Leader/Sponsor_____

Places Visited_____
_____
_____
_____

Memorable Events_____
_____
_____
_____

Wildlife Sightings_____
_____
_____

Expenses *(Lodging/Dining/Fees)*_____
_____
_____

Surprises_____
_____
_____

Itinerary for this trip is on page _____   **Journal contunued on page** _____

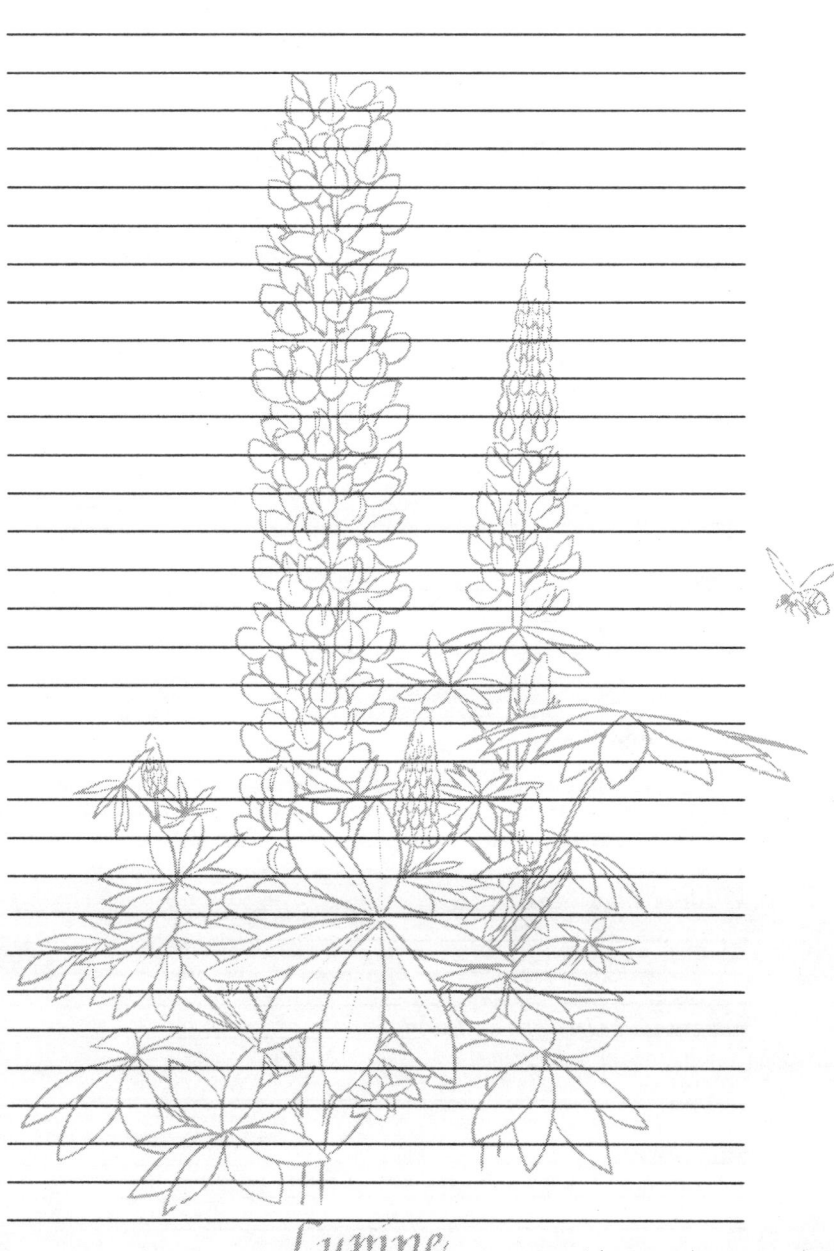

Journal

TRAVEL RECORD

My Trip To _____

Description_____
_____

Dates_____
              Leave   *Return*
Weather_____
_____

Mode of Travel _____ Mileage_____

Companions_____
_____

Leader/Sponsor_____

Places Visited_____
_____
_____
_____

Memorable Events_____
_____
_____
_____

Wildlife Sightings_____
_____
_____

Expenses *(Lodging/Dining/Fees)*_____
_____
_____

Surprises_____
_____
_____

Itinerary for this trip is on page _____   Journal contunued on page _____

Journal

> *Life is either a daring ADVENTURE or nothing.*
> — Helen Keller

TRAVEL RECORD

My Trip To _____

Description _____
_____

Dates _____
          Leave   Return
Weather _____
_____

Mode of Travel _____ Mileage _____

Companions _____
_____

Leader/Sponsor _____

Places Visited _____
_____
_____
_____

Memorable Events _____
_____
_____
_____

Wildlife Sightings _____
_____
_____

Expenses *(Lodging/Dining/Fees)* _____
_____
_____

Surprises _____
_____
_____

Itinerary for this trip is on page _____   Journal contunued on page _____

Journal

Great Blue Heron

TRAVEL RECORD

My Trip To _____

Description _____
_____

Dates _____
    Leave   Return

Weather _____
_____

Mode of Travel _____ Mileage _____

Companions _____
_____

Leader/Sponsor _____

Places Visited _____
_____
_____
_____

Memorable Events _____
_____
_____
_____

Wildlife Sightings _____
_____
_____

Expenses *(Lodging/Dining/Fees)* _____
_____
_____

Surprises _____
_____
_____

Itinerary for this trip is on page _____ Journal contunued on page _____

Journal

Page 43

Be patient.
In time, grass becomes milk.

Anon.

TRAVEL RECORD

My Trip To _____

Description _____
_____

Dates _____
    Leave   Return
Weather _____
_____

Mode of Travel _____ Mileage _____

Companions _____
_____

Leader/Sponsor _____

Places Visited _____
_____
_____
_____
_____

Memorable Events _____
_____
_____
_____
_____

Wildlife Sightings _____
_____
_____
_____

Expenses *(Lodging/Dining/Fees)* _____
_____
_____
_____

Surprises _____
_____
_____

Itinerary for this trip is on page _____ Journal contunued on page _____

Journal

Bear

TRAVEL RECORD

My Trip To _____

Description _____
_____

Dates _____
           Leave   Return
Weather _____
_____

Mode of Travel _____ Mileage _____

Companions _____
_____

Leader/Sponsor _____

Places Visited _____
_____
_____
_____

Memorable Events _____
_____
_____
_____

Wildlife Sightings _____
_____
_____

Expenses *(Lodging/Dining/Fees)* _____
_____
_____

Surprises _____
_____
_____

Itinerary for this trip is on page _____   **Journal contunued on page** _____

Journal

> The only cats worth anything are the cats who TAKE CHANCES
>
> — Theolonius Monk

TRAVEL RECORD

My Trip To _____

Description _____
_____

Dates _____
           Leave   Return

Weather _____
_____

Mode of Travel _____ Mileage _____

Companions _____
_____

Leader/Sponsor _____

Places Visited _____
_____
_____
_____

Memorable Events _____
_____
_____
_____

Wildlife Sightings _____
_____
_____

Expenses *(Lodging/Dining/Fees)* _____
_____
_____

Surprises _____
_____
_____

Itinerary for this trip is on page _____   Journal contunued on page _____

Journal

Page 49

TRAVEL RECORD

My Trip To _____

Description _____
_____

Dates _____
             Leave   Return
Weather _____
_____

Mode of Travel _____ Mileage _____

Companions _____
_____

Leader/Sponsor _____

Places Visited _____
_____
_____
_____

Memorable Events _____
_____
_____
_____

Wildlife Sightings _____
_____
_____

Expenses *(Lodging/Dining/Fees)* _____
_____
_____

Surprises _____
_____
_____

Itinerary for this trip is on page _____   Journal contunued on page _____

Journal

> *My heart is tuned
> to the quietness
> that the stillness
> of nature inspires.*
>
> Hazrat Inayat Khan

TRAVEL RECORD

My Trip To _____

Description _____
_____

Dates _____
        Leave   Return
Weather _____
_____

Mode of Travel _____ Mileage _____

Companions _____
_____

Leader/Sponsor _____

Places Visited _____
_____
_____
_____

Memorable Events _____
_____
_____
_____

Wildlife Sightings _____
_____
_____

Expenses *(Lodging/Dining/Fees)* _____
_____
_____

Surprises _____
_____
_____

Itinerary for this trip is on page _____   Journal contunued on page _____

Journal

Water-lily

Page 54

TRAVEL RECORD

My Trip To _____

Description _____
_____

Dates _____
             Leave   Return
Weather _____
_____

Mode of Travel _____ Mileage _____

Companions _____
_____

Leader/Sponsor _____

Places Visited _____
_____
_____
_____

Memorable Events _____
_____
_____
_____
_____

Wildlife Sightings _____
_____
_____

Expenses *(Lodging/Dining/Fees)* _____
_____
_____
_____

Surprises _____
_____
_____

Itinerary for this trip is on page _____   Journal contunued on page _____

Journal

Never try to catch two FROGS with one hand.

Chinese Proverb

TRAVEL RECORD

My Trip To _____

Description_____

Dates_____
           Leave   Return

Weather_____

Mode of Travel _____ Mileage_____

Companions_____

Leader/Sponsor_____

Places Visited_____
_____
_____
_____

Memorable Events_____
_____
_____
_____

Wildlife Sightings_____
_____
_____

Expenses *(Lodging/Dining/Fees)*_____
_____
_____

Surprises_____
_____
_____

Itinerary for this trip is on page _____   Journal contunued on page _____

Journal

Porcupine

TRAVEL RECORD

My Trip To _____

Description_____
_____

Dates_____
        Leave   Return

Weather_____
_____

Mode of Travel _____ Mileage_____

Companions_____
_____

Leader/Sponsor_____

Places Visited_____
_____
_____
_____

Memorable Events_____
_____
_____
_____

Wildlife Sightings_____
_____
_____

Expenses *(Lodging/Dining/Fees)*_____
_____
_____

Surprises_____
_____
_____

Itinerary for this trip is on page _____   **Journal contunued on page _____**

Journal

Columbia River Petroglyph

If I had influence
with the good fairy
who is supposed to preside over
the christening of all children,
I should ask
that her gift to each child in the
world be a
Sense of Wonder
so indestructible that it would
last a lifetime.

Rachel Carson

Ideas For Your Journal

Peak Experiences: *The highest or utmost point of anything... write down your peak experiences today for later recall.*

The following pages are for extending information from the Travel Record & Journal pages. Be creative & include:
- stories, incidents, lists
- sketches, drawings
- photographs, maps, trail markings
- feathers, leaf samples, rubbings
- notes to remember for the next trip

Make your journal valuable:
- write about your fun as well as foibles (weaknesses)
- write in this journal often
- use accurate, detailed descriptions
- sensory words (feelings, smells, tastes, etc.)
- ask others on the trip how they remember events, collaborate on your stories
- fill the open space with keepsakes or sketches
- draw a map to a secret waterfall or hot spring
- make notations about what to bring next time

Outdoor Tips
- Don't wear cotton under your raingear. Wool or a synthetic will keep you dry & comfortable.
- Try burning a small candle in your tent before bedtime to raise the temperature and lower humidity.
- Peanut butter is a good snack for hikers. It is high in fats, protein and carbohydrates.
- If you become lost, go downhill. You'll find people living in valleys, roads and water.
- Don't drink water from streams. Boil water at least 20 minutes before drinking.

Journal Continued from Travel Record page _____

Keepsake / Sketch

Page 63

Continued from Travel Record page ——   *Journal*

The word is picnic, not nitpick.

Lloyd J. Reynolds

Journal   Continued from Travel Record page _____

Keepsake / Sketch

Continued from Travel Record page _____ *Journal*

Dragonfly

Journal Continued from Travel Record page _____

Keepsake / Sketch

Continued from Travel Record page ———   *Journal*

> *Beware of all enterprises that require new clothes.*
>
> THOREAU

Journal Continued from Travel Record page _____

Keepsake / Sketch

Continued from Travel Record page _____

Journal

Chestnut-sided Warbler

Journal Continued from Travel Record page _____

Keepsake / Sketch

Continued from Travel Record page _____   *Journal*

> When the bird & the book disagree, always believe the bird.
>
> — Birdwatchers Proverb

Journal Continued from Travel Record page _____

Keepsake / Sketch

Page 73

Continued from Travel Record page _____   *Journal*

Wild Lupine

Journal Continued from Travel Record page _____

Keepsake / Sketch

Continued from Travel Record page _____ *Journal*

*I finally got it
all together
& I forgot where I put it.*

—Anon.

Journal   Continued from Travel Record page _____

Keepsake / Sketch

Continued from Travel Record page _____ *Journal*

Page 78

Journal Continued from Travel Record page _____

Keepsake / Sketch

Continued from Travel Record page ____ *Journal*

No matter how wet & cold you are, you're always warm & dry on the inside.

Woodsman's Adage

Journal Continued from Travel Record page _____

Keepsake / Sketch

Continued from Travel Record page _____   *Journal*

Page 82

Journal Continued from Travel Record page _____

Keepsake / Sketch

Continued from Travel Record page ____   *Journal*

The butterfly even when persued, never appears in a hurry.

Garaku

The real voyage
of
DISCOVERY
consists not in
seeking new landscapes, but in
having new eyes.

Marcel Proust

Using the Trip Planner-Itinerary

The facing pages are intended to be used together for planning your trip. Include such details as:
- Day/Date
- Important Phone Numbers
- Planned Activities
- Expenses
- Contacts
- Lodging & Confirmation Number

Trip Planner - Itinerary

Companions	Barbara, Brooke, Sarah, Mike
Costs	Accomodations, Phones, Etc.

Day 1 — Mountain Resort Hotel
$85 per nite   1-800-555-1212

Day 2 — Mtn. Resort Hotel
$85 per, $40/person — River Raft Reservation

Day 3 — Set up
$12 nite   1-5...

Day 4 — Camp...
567-8910 Dinner

Day 5 — Stay...
1-503...

Day 6 — Bac...

Day 7

Trip Planner - Itinerary

My Trip to **Central Oregon**

Day/Date	Planned Activities
Day 1 Monday July 26	Drive to Bend, check in to Resort Hotel, Relax! Bike trip
Day 2 Tues. July 27	River rafting, Horseback riding, Lunching - Tennis
Day 3 Wed. July 28	Check out of hotel, Drive to campsite, Set up tent/trailer - fishing
Day 4 Thurs July 29	Go to see Lava Caves, Hiking - Biking
Day 5 Friday July 30	Sight seeing local area, Drive to Eugene to visit with family
Day 6 Sat. July 31	Trip home, unpack
Day 7	

Trip Planner - Itinerary

My Trip to _____

Day/Date	Planned Activities
Day 1	
Day 2	
Day 3	
Day 4	
Day 5	
Day 6	
Day 7	

Trip Planner - Itinerary

Companions _____

| Costs | Accomodations, Phones, Etc. |

Day 1

Day 2

Day 3

Day 4

Day 5

Day 6

Day 7

Trip Planner - Itinerary

My Trip to _____

Day/Date	Planned Activities

Day 1

Day 2

Day 3

Day 4

Day 5

Day 6

Day 7

Trip Planner - Itinerary

Companions _____

Costs	Accomodations, Phones, Etc.

Day 1

Day 2

Day 3

Day 4

Day 5

Day 6

Day 7

Trip Planner - Itinerary

My Trip to _____

| Day/Date | Planned Activities |

Day 1
_____
_____

Day 2
_____
_____

Day 3
_____
_____

Day 4
_____
_____

Day 5
_____
_____

Day 6
_____
_____

Day 7
_____
_____

Trip Planner - Itinerary

Companions _____

   Costs   Accomodations, Phones, Etc.

Day 1

Day 2

Day 3

Day 4

Day 5

Day 6

Day 7

Trip Planner - Itinerary

My Trip to _____

Day/Date	Planned Activities
Day 1	
Day 2	
Day 3	
Day 4	
Day 5	
Day 6	
Day 7	

Trip Planner - Itinerary

Companions _____

Costs   Accomodations, Phones, Etc.

Day 1

Day 2

Day 3

Day 4

Day 5

Day 6

Day 7

Belted Kingfisher

1994

January 1994
S	M	T	W	T	F	S
						1
2	3	4	5	6	7	8
9	10	11	12	13	14	15
16	17	18	19	20	21	22
23	24	25	26	27	28	29
30	31					

February 1994
S	M	T	W	T	F	S
		1	2	3	4	5
6	7	8	9	10	11	12
13	14	15	16	17	18	19
20	21	22	23	24	25	26
27	28					

March 1994
S	M	T	W	T	F	S
		1	2	3	4	5
6	7	8	9	10	11	12
13	14	15	16	17	18	19
20	21	22	23	24	25	26
27	28	29	30	31		

April 1994
S	M	T	W	T	F	S
					1	2
3	4	5	6	7	8	9
10	11	12	13	14	15	16
17	18	19	20	21	22	23
24	25	26	27	28	29	30

May 1994
S	M	T	W	T	F	S
1	2	3	4	5	6	7
8	9	10	11	12	13	14
15	16	17	18	19	20	21
22	23	24	25	26	27	28
29	30	31				

June 1994
S	M	T	W	T	F	S
			1	2	3	4
5	6	7	8	9	10	11
12	13	14	15	16	17	18
19	20	21	22	23	24	25
26	27	28	29	30		

July 1994
S	M	T	W	T	F	S
					1	2
3	4	5	6	7	8	9
10	11	12	13	14	15	16
17	18	19	20	21	22	23
24	25	26	27	28	29	30
31						

August 1994
S	M	T	W	T	F	S
	1	2	3	4	5	6
7	8	9	10	11	12	13
14	15	16	17	18	19	20
21	22	23	24	25	26	27
28	29	30	31			

September 1994
S	M	T	W	T	F	S
				1	2	3
4	5	6	7	8	9	10
11	12	13	14	15	16	17
18	19	20	21	22	23	24
25	26	27	28	29	30	

October 1994
S	M	T	W	T	F	S
						1
2	3	4	5	6	7	8
9	10	11	12	13	14	15
16	17	18	19	20	21	22
23	24	25	26	27	28	29
30	31					

November 1994
S	M	T	W	T	F	S
		1	2	3	4	5
6	7	8	9	10	11	12
13	14	15	16	17	18	19
20	21	22	23	24	25	26
27	28	29	30			

December 1994
S	M	T	W	T	F	S
				1	2	3
4	5	6	7	8	9	10
11	12	13	14	15	16	17
18	19	20	21	22	23	24
25	26	27	28	29	30	31

1995

January 1995
S	M	T	W	T	F	S
1	2	3	4	5	6	7
8	9	10	11	12	13	14
15	16	17	18	19	20	21
22	23	24	25	26	27	28
29	30	31				

February 1995
S	M	T	W	T	F	S
			1	2	3	4
5	6	7	8	9	10	11
12	13	14	15	16	17	18
19	20	21	22	23	24	25
26	27	28				

March 1995
S	M	T	W	T	F	S
			1	2	3	4
5	6	7	8	9	10	11
12	13	14	15	16	17	18
19	20	21	22	23	24	25
26	27	28	29	30	31	

April 1995
S	M	T	W	T	F	S
						1
2	3	4	5	6	7	8
9	10	11	12	13	14	15
16	17	18	19	20	21	22
23	24	25	26	27	28	29
30						

May 1995
S	M	T	W	T	F	S
	1	2	3	4	5	6
7	8	9	10	11	12	13
14	15	16	17	18	19	20
21	22	23	24	25	26	27
28	29	30	31			

June 1995
S	M	T	W	T	F	S
				1	2	3
4	5	6	7	8	9	10
11	12	13	14	15	16	17
18	19	20	21	22	23	24
25	26	27	28	29	30	

July 1995
S	M	T	W	T	F	S
						1
2	3	4	5	6	7	8
9	10	11	12	13	14	15
16	17	18	19	20	21	22
23	24	25	26	27	28	29
30	31					

August 1995
S	M	T	W	T	F	S
		1	2	3	4	5
6	7	8	9	10	11	12
13	14	15	16	17	18	19
20	21	22	23	24	25	26
27	28	29	30	31		

September 1995
S	M	T	W	T	F	S
					1	2
3	4	5	6	7	8	9
10	11	12	13	14	15	16
17	18	19	20	21	22	23
24	25	26	27	28	29	30

October 1995
S	M	T	W	T	F	S
1	2	3	4	5	6	7
8	9	10	11	12	13	14
15	16	17	18	19	20	21
22	23	24	25	26	27	28
29	30	31				

November 1995
S	M	T	W	T	F	S
			1	2	3	4
5	6	7	8	9	10	11
12	13	14	15	16	17	18
19	20	21	22	23	24	25
26	27	28	29	30		

December 1995
S	M	T	W	T	F	S
					1	2
3	4	5	6	7	8	9
10	11	12	13	14	15	16
17	18	19	20	21	22	23
24	25	26	27	28	29	30
31						

To Order:
Please contact your local bookstore,
outdoor or travel store,
or write to us at

AHA Calligraphy / QCC, Inc.
PEAK EXPERIENCES
P.O. Box 2128
Beaverton, OR 97075-2128

Completed on this 9th day of July, 1993
on 60 # Offset Book, vellum finish
in Adobe Garamond with
reverance for the great
outdoors.
❦